THE DOCTOR OF MY EYE

THE MAGIC OF LOVE..!

HAYFORD BOADI

PROLOGUE

'Shekyna.' He pauses and takes a breath. 'You are beautiful and I like you a lot. I can't stop thinking about you from the first day I saw you. I know this is insane but I needed to tell you there is something about you that is so attractive I can't let go.

Shekyna a young beautiful lady who happens to spot love as the saying goes "love at first sight" and Naruk a young handsome medical doctor who also having the same crush on her. Will the magic of love magnetized them.....?

THE DOCTOR OF MY EYE

~~~~~SHEKYNA~~~~~~

I stare at the wall again but this time the sharpness in my stare is intense. It penetrates the body lying lifeless in front of me to the wall and beyond it. My eyes squint at each thought that takes its turn in my head.

I shouldn't be thinking about this, this is the kind of thing to be shrugged off as insignificant but it manages to bother me to the point of nausea. I don't even realize it until now when my head is refusing to comply with any form of reasoning. My head continue rolling in involuntary contemplation making me despise myself. I hate that I hate thinking about this and the bitterness runs on.

I bite a corner of my lower lip, I bite it so hard that it gets to the edge of bleeding but it doesn't bleed, the voice that saves it beats the snot out of me. I let it loose.

'What time is it?' he asks as he brings himself back to the world of the living. He tries to pull his weight up the pillow placed horizontally beneath him but the pain surging from his broken left leg, broken left arm sandwiched in a POP and bandaged head overwhelms him so much that he eventually gives up, lying still again, his body lifeless, the little life in him only showing from the eyes he just opened and the silent sounds his lips are making.

His accident was unfair, *considering* it was an actual accident. In my opinion, it was a failed attempt at homicide leaving the man lying in front of me, who is my father, severely fractured.

The doctor who performed his surgery said the car that runs over him broke him way beyond what a man his age can handle. That fed the resentment collected inside me which I had since then
~~~~~

felt for whoever was responsible to satisfaction. If only he hadn't escaped, I'm sure to have ripped his throat out instantly. One witness said 'he didn't even stop to see if he had hit a human being or a thing, he drove off in speed like nothing happened.'

'It's 4:40pm.' came my reply as I lean forward on the edge of the chair, my hands gripping the raised siderail of his bed, to observe him. He has been knocked out for the past twelve hours on anesthesia and he finally awakes. At least.

I want to ask him if he would eat or drink anything but the doctor has been strict on his warning to only feed him an hour after he is awake so I pick up my phone instead and dial my mother's number. She is not here because she's home putting together a meal.The excitement in her voice is like fuel to my own excitement. As we converse, I smile so wide my lips begin to shudder until I remember 'I have to call the doctor to come check if everything is smooth' and I hang up.

For a split second I forgot my worries, which didn't last longer than a minute because, as I jerk up,it comes smashing into me again hard enough that I almost fall back into the chair. I manage to gather myself and I start outin search of the one person I wished I'd rather not deal with.

Fear gripped me as soon as my eyes find him on a couch inside the doctors' office, sending an emergency signal to my limbs to vibrate. The sweats drenching my palms begin to drip so I rub them together and clear my throat. His eyes find me and he stands.

He's wearing a grey shirt over blue jeans submerged under his white coat and I must admit, though reluctantly, that he is a fine blend of handsome. As I walk closer to him, I notice the similarity in the shirt he's wearing to the one he wore on the day a bizarre encounter ensued between us.

~~~~~~~~

I was at the counter to settle my father's surgery bill when our eyes
~~~~~~~~

met for the first time that day. I was captivated by his good looks so it wasn't unusual for me to be found wanting in speech. He had looked at me for a split second and, having asked for the umpteenth time what he could do for me without any response, seized the sheet of paper that was hanging loosely in my hand. I struggled to gain composure.

'Please lady, have you paid your bill at the accounts office?' he asked politely after examining it.

'Yes.' I reverted. There was confusion registered on his face as the mouse he dragged took him several places on the desktop computer. He then called the accounts office, I deduced, to confirm the suspicions he had.

'Your bill has not fully been paid.' The surprise must have done a big number on me though I tried to not act the part. He simply shrugged. My Uncle had promised to clear the medical bill the last time he visited, he is not the kind of man who would say 'I will take care of it' and not do, so I was utterly surprised at his statement.

'Oh! Isn't there something we can do to push through with the surgery in the meantime?' I said aloud as I decided to not call my Uncle straight away. If he said he will take care of it, he will.

He nods, goes to a cabinet and retrieves a sheet.

'You can sign this document but you'll need a guarantor, someone who works here as a nurse or a doctor.' He handed me the document.

'But I don't know any doctor or nurse here. Kindly help me out.' I cried. He looked at me pointedly and then said 'Well lady, I can't help you.'

'Please, I promise you, it will be handled by the close of today. You see, his surgery is tomorrow and the preparations have to start immediately. That can't happen if he is not cleared, please.' I begged. He could sense the sincerity in my words so he agreed but went on to explain, 'There have been several cases where a doctor or a nurse had their neck on the line because they took pity on someone and guaranteed for their patient. Please do not disappoint me.' He begged 'Sign here!' and added. I nervously took the pen and signed mechanically. He turned it to the back and transcribed his own signature on a given space. Looking at me, he said, 'That will be all for now.' I wagged my head before I walked out.

Though my uncle eventually settled the rest of the bill, I could still not seem to take it off my mind because I was embarrassed. I hate that all I have been doing since then has been continuously playing the incident in my head and avoiding him at all costs. But here I am in front of him again and I'm dumfounded.

~~~~~~~~~

If glasses were ever intended to match the DNA of a person, it's now I'm only finding out because the one on him agrees with everything that makes up his being. He has a peculiar ability of increasing the aesthetic degree of the things that come upon his body.

'Yes?' He walks closer and draws his ear to me to show he's listening.

'M-my dad is awake.' I stammer my response.

Without saying another word, he grabs his stethoscope and signals for me to lead the way but when we are outside the room he walks ahead as I follow closely behind, my eyes lowered to the shoals of his feet.

Momentarily, my attention is robbed by a scene between a hysterical patient and a nurse on the hallway while I'm still walking, it's incredible how pain can drive mad a person, I thought. Before I had a chance to stop my steps though, my face is already on his chest because he has also just stopped to watch, my heart skips a beat.
~~~~~~~~~

~~~~~~~NARUK~~~~~~

Hectic is an understatement sitting at the counter most parts of my days as the doctor-in-charge. Although I love my job, to deal directly with both patients and their caretakers sometimes can be the misery of my life. We have been taught in medical school to harbor patience and keep the smiles on our faces gleaming in all conditions, you know, being compassionate and all, I understand the necessity of that because the excruciating pain and suffering that looms this ward day-in and day-out is misery personified. Not much words can describe the agony both patients and their loved ones go through when admitted at this specific ward.

Sometimes I wish there was an easier way to make the pain go away faster but the rule is, to relieve them of the pain, they must be put through even more acute pain before it all begins to heal. The healing as it is does not take a day or two or three or even a month or two or three, it takes real time. Each day a step ahead as it fades but never completely flashing out. And the scars become a permanent reminder of the agony.

Working in pair with Juliana at the counter gives this hardship a touch of fun. She is elaborately comical and jovial. She can examine a serious scenario and make it laughable, though not in a cynical way.

The payment I have to make for this somewhat entertaining personality is to endure her bullying. Not a single day goes by without her chanting about her believe that every single young lady at the hospital has a *thing* for me and her usual coy wink parceling her assumptions makes me want to cry out of exaggerated frustration.

Although it is true my good-looks precede my reputation, it is still too surreal to think I can be the center of attraction to every lady in a big place like this. During one of our many heart-to-heart talks, I mentioned my status as a single man, which I regretted immediately because I gave away to her the ultimate yardstick to put herself on a mission to find me a perfect match.
~~~~~~~

Juliana: 'Look, Naruk, I have always known I have a purpose in your life. But I could never guess it is this big a thing.' She emphatically says.

Me: 'Just forget it, please, jolly.' I beg in frustration referring to her by the pet name I coined to suit her cheerful, upbeat nature.

Juliana: 'You can't talk me out of it.' came her reply with all seriousness.

Me: 'Please just do your job and forget this. I'm not ready.' I'm still pleading as I say but she pretends not to be listening.

Juliana: 'Well, that's too bad because whether you're ready or not, I'm like a bug that sucks its host dry, I'm not giving up on you. Besides, where else would you meet someone when you are always hooked on your work?' Her voice becomes softer as she speaks. I then begin to feel this is important to her. I pursue the matter no further.

I have had friends in the past. Unfortunately, respecting the boundaries of male and female friendships was not always in their books with me, they wanted benefits, all the time, some I could afford to render, those inclined towards intimate bindings I succinctly rejected.

Juliana is different, she is the first female friend I made in the hospital who genuinely was interested in being *just friends*. She saw beyond the wall I built around myself to cage out the world; the seriousness, the strictness and the hardness. Unlike the rest who endure me, in our case, I'm the one doing the enduring. And this 'enduring' has transformed my social life in many ways than I can possibly count. If I'd say appreciation is the best I can do for her friendship, I'd be devaluing it.

It has been over a week since she set out on her feat of wife-finding for me. We are into our second week of duty and so far, it doesn't seem to me she is ever going to stop at nothing. It wouldn't be Juliana if she did. As she keeps snatching my attention towards the numerous ladies that pour in and out of the ward each day, I, eventually, set my eyes on *a girl.*

~~~~~~~~~~~

First of all, I don't ever stare at anyone more than a minute. But as I watched her follow the scoop stretcher being pushed by two nurses into the ward, her peach floral dress hanging loosely on her slim figure, gripping her at the waist and a cream veil tided-up in a turban on her head, my eyes wanted to be nowhere else.
As I sit in my office behind the glass window shielding her from my piercing glances for the past three days, she eventually made her way to me *that day.*

Fast-forward to this moment she's in my arms. Although it's only her head leaning on my chest, I feel every nerve that would have awaken if this was a hug awakening. It didn't occur to me she was walking as closely behind as I made a quick one-eighty to observe the commotion erupting at the back.

I suddenly don't remember why I turned or where I was heading before I had to turn or my name or where I come from. Everything escapes me. I sallow, blink, apologize and vanish into the ward.
~~~~~~~~~~~

~~~~~~SHEKYNA~~~~~~

I walk sluggishly into the ward room my father shares with four other patients who have either their leg broken, arm broken or both. His bed is besides a window at one of the four corners in the room. I drag the curtain partitioning to one side and spot my mom arranging some toiletries in a cardboard. My father is awake leaning on a pillow, from the look of things, he has just eaten. He looks more alive than he was two weeks ago.

'Ehen! Shekyna, you are here. I brought food for you too. Check the green bowl in the basket there.' She points at the basket at her back while faced forward. 'Push it to me let me take out those fruits. Asana sent them for your father but knowing your love for fruits, I must hide them. I sincerely hope you don't finish them before your father is able to eat them.' She looks at me suspiciously pursing her lips as I burst out laughing. She is right.

But I'm not only laughing because she has a point, I do also because my heart is glad that she is sane enough to make jokes.

A week ago, my father was not responding so well to treatment after his surgery, we were all sad. No one was talking or eating properly as the worse was expected. But into the second week, things took on a new turn, *'I guess the treatment needed time to manifest. He is recovering well.'*the doctor had announced igniting
~~~~~~

our hope. And it has been progress since then.

I wipe a few drops of tears snaking down my face that accompanied the laughter and say 'As you are putting them in that drawer be sure to lock it too before what we don't both want happens, you know I'm not the only fruit person who lingers about here.'

I say above her shoulder when she kneels to secure a place for it. Just then Nagim and Naza, the stubborn pair I have for siblings, walk in to hear the screeching sound of the drawer closing. They've grown too big for their seventeen years of age. The difference in age between us might be six years but as they stand beside me, I begin to doubt the credibility of that fact. 'Talk of the little devils!' I roll my eyes at them.

Nagim, the boy, walks past me with his lips stretched out in rebellion as he walks to grab my mom's arm, 'Mama, what is in the black polythene you just put there? It is smelling like bananas.' He says with a childish giggle. She shakes him off and replies, 'Go and sit down!' I laugh. For the first time, we hear my father snigger, we all laugh.

When the laughter subsides, Naza walks to his siderail and pulls it down, she jumps and sits on the edge of the bed by his side and starts whispering to him about her day. The way she is seated exposes how very identical she is to her twin brother, in that posture, she could be mistaken for him.

There is still a shadow over me so I feel there must be someone else behind me. I turn with my whole body and he was standing there, two inches above me in blue jeans over a green T-shirt with the inscriptions **'I'll survive'** boldly written across the length of it. His white coat is partially burying his outfit and for the first time, I notice his name - Ahmed Naruk Junior - weaved in tiny letters on the left side of his white coat, perpendicular to his heart, the same spot it tinges within me whenever I think about him.

He smiles nodding at my mom, at my dad and at me. Even though his presence has suddenly taken up all the air in the room, I manage to pull off a smile at least.

'Waw! There's so much life in here!' he says smiling and gently claps his hands together such that he doesn't make a sound.' He must have been standing there for a while. I thought.

'Yes doctor, by God's grace we are laughing again. Would you imagine last week by this time we were....' and she goes on to narrate every single detail of the trauma we went through as if the doctor she was talking to isn't the same doctor who saw us through it all. Sometimes I wonder how she found my father; quiet, calm and reserved, being such a chatterbox.

I roll my eyes at all that she is saying while I pretend I'm not completely mesmerized by his smile as he's smiling a lot at my mom talking.

'Hahaaa!' She laughs heartily to mark the end of her narration. 'Anyway, you are welcome. How are you doctor?'

'I'm well, Ma.' he replies.

'Ehen, why is it that every day we are buying one medicine or the other even with our Insurance? Does that thing work at all?' Her tone becomes serious. 'And if it's not spending money here and there on medicines, it's walking up and down to do only-God-knows-what, eih, can't you people be a little organized? I'm lucky to have my smart and vibrant daughter right there....' She winks at me, he turns and throws a flash glance at me as well, and I feign typing something on my phone so I don't catch his gaze.

I know what my mom is trying to do with her specific diction and I'm not falling for it. She has been buying me new clothes and encouraging me to dress up since my father began recovery, 'A lady must look her best all the time because you don't know whom you might just attract.' she had explained but we both knew she was doing that because her life-long dream of having a doctor son-in-law might just come true.

'Well, errm, that is how the system is. Even we doctors wished something could be done about it. Hmm! Anyways, I'm here to see if he's properly responding to treatment. As usual I'll need all of you to excuse me, if you don't mind.' he says.

'Oh Yes, we were just leaving. Nagim go and greet your father and let's go. Quickly, quickly! Naza get down from there and give your brother space.' she says while she picks the basket and takes out the green bowl. I wonder what food she cooked because I'm starving. Unfortunately, food will have to wait. I follow them to leave when he says 'you can stay'. I pause.'I mean I need one person around.' he tries to explain. I'm facing him now and our eyes are locked into each other. There's something in the way he is looking at me, something in it that is similar to the way I'm looking at him. He pulls away first as he walks to the drip stand on the side of the bed.

It's just him, me and my half asleep father as the drips start to work their power on him. He eventually falls asleep. It's just him and me now, in this space, away from the world's eye. The awkwardness begins to suffocate me so I pull a chair by the drawer and sit. He is busy injecting some medicines in the drips and I watch him with the corner of my eye. *He's so handsome.* He opens the bandage on my father's thigh slightly and flinches at something he sees, I become alert so I get up and walk to where he's standing and I see the blood soaking the sheets, his wound is open.

'We need to clean this up. Go to the....never mind.' he realizes that whatever he was about to send me on an errand for will reach him faster if he does it himself. He bolts out and comes back with a surgical kit, drawing the curtain partitioning closer than before.

~~~~~~~~

I'm still standing at my spot besides him so I can see inside the box when he opens it. There's a surgical blade, needle, thread, bandages, an ointment and a colorless liquid I can't make out.
~~~~~~~~

'Are you going to perform a mini-surgery here?' I ask frightened. 'No. I'm just going to close his wound. By the way, I'll need your help. Hold this.' He hands me the bandages and I begin to unwrap them. I watch him stitch the open wound meticulously, his hands steady and his sight focused, while I wince at each thread that goes in and comes out.

He finishes and cleans it up with the colorless liquid before rubbing the ointment on him. He looks at my hand, seeing that I have prepared the bandages for plastering he says, 'Good. Put them on the wound.' He is tearing a plaster as he speaks, I'm flustered by his 'Good' but I immediately bring my head down from the cloud and concentrate. My hand is holding the bandages at both ends across the wound as he plaster them one after the other, our hands touching each time. I try not to feel the excitement filling me as our hands touch. *I'm really trying.* Just when I manage to hold it together, he brings his hand around my back to my father's knee where there is another wound, my back is against his front, his face on my shoulder and his hands caging me between him. 'What is your name?' he whispers. *I can't breath.*

'Shekyna. My name is Shekyna.' I say choking on my own saliva.

'Okay, Shekyna. Tell me, how old are you?'

'Twenty-three.'

'You married.'

'No.'

'Boyfriend?'

'Nope. I'm single.' I quickly added, regretting it instantly but I can feel his jaw widening on my shoulder, he is smiling. He likes that I'm single. But why?

We are still pegged together as his hand is working on the wound on my father's knee. If anyone was to walk in on us, they'd think he's hugging me from the back. I stand still, frozen. My hands lifted to my chest in a fist. His breathing is on my neck, his body completely burying me. He can feel the tension consuming me so he tells me to 'relax!', smiling again. *I can't relax.*

All this while, my father is sound asleep. He doesn't even stir while his wound was being stitched. I begin to wonder what medicines he injected in the drips to knock him out entirely. He eventually finishes the patches on the knee wound. I wait for him to pull away for me to 'relax' like he suggested but he doesn't, instead, he draws even closer into me in a hug and holds my hands in front of me, my fists tighten.

'Shekyna.' He pauses and takes a breath. 'You are beautiful and I like you a lot. I can't stop thinking about you from the first day I saw you. I know this is insane but I needed to tell you there is something about you that is so attractive I can't let go. This is my number.' He pulls my phone from my pocket, it isn't locked because the screen is still on, he types in ten digits and saves it as Naruk. 'Text me tonight when you are free. I will be expecting it.' he let go of my hands and leaves. Just. Like. That.

I am still frozen at the same position he left me for over five minutes when a nurse walks in. She says she has come to pick the surgical kit so I move for her to do that. She does just that and leaves. I'm back in the chair and I keep staring down at my phone, his name is on my screen. *Naruk, Naruk, Naruk....* I repeat it countless times because it sounds even better each time.

~~~~~~~NARUK~~~~~~~~

I put the stethoscope to my patient's heart for the second time hoping this time I will be able to hear the beats of his heart but all I can hear is the clock ticking. Tic tok, tic tok. I shake my head to clear it. The nurse standing by me can sense I'm distracted by something, there is bewilderment written on her face as she obviously has never seen me like this in the one and a half years she has been working at this hospital.
The clock on the wall strikes ten pm and I tell her to inject the patient, a young-man of about thirty-one, whose blood pressure shot to the roof due to the acute pain he is barely enduring, with morphine to put him to sleep, 'that will do for now. 'I say absent-mindedly walking out the door, my speed increasing at each step until I'm pacing towards my office where my phone is.

Since the minute I left her transfixed to the ground like a statue, I have been counting down the minutes to the time when I could finally attend to my phone, to her message. However, as I'm pacing down the hallway to my office, I can't deny any longer the anxiety expounding within me.What if she doesn't feel the same way?
~~~~~~~

What if she never texts? What if....?

I stand over my phone staring down at it on my desk, my hands holding my waist, observing it closely as if that is how to eliminate all doubts. I eventually decide to pick it up and switch it on, I flip it twice arriving at the screen where I can locate the WhatsApp icon and I place my thump on it in a tap. It opens. I wait for a few minutes for my messages to load but nothing was happening. I grow restless, my heart rate palpitating vigorously.

I take off my coat and eye-glasses and gently throw both on the table, the eye-glasses landing on the coat. As I take my seat, I notice my Wi-Fi icon is not blue like it should be if it's on. I take a deep breath and impulsively turn it on. The messages begin to load. I scroll through as they load, most of them are from groups, a few from my patients, and one new message from an alien contact. I open it. It isn't her.

I sit pensively considering all the reasons that might be keeping her from texting me yet or ever. It stings like a bee in my chest. I don't know what to feel or how to feel it. So rather than brood all night in my office, I pack my stuff and go home.

Upon reaching home, I pack my car haphazardly. I was a particularly meticulous young man before the moment my heart was possibly broken. It is now eleven-twenty pm, I can feel the exhaustion, emotional rather than physical, as I walk through the front door into my two bedroom apartment. The cleaner must have come around because the hall is sparkling. I can smell something delicious from the kitchen, her cooking, but I've lost my appetite. I dump my keys on the three inches flat screen TV stand, following it with my phone and that was when I saw the message I have been waiting for all night.

'Hello, Doctor. This is Shekyna.'

I rush for the phone, reverting her message immediately.

'Hi, dear. I'm glad you texted. I went almost crazy waiting for your message.' No, that might scare her. I delete the message in the text box and type again. 'Hi, Shekyna. I'm glad you texted. Just call me Naruk, would you please?' Send!

Shekyna Typing...

'Okay. Naruk. How was your day?'

Naruk typing...

'Adventurous, to say the least. Lemme guess, your day was tiring.'

Shekyna typing....

'Tiring, yes. Also very shocking.'

Naruk typing...

'Tell me about it.'

Shekyna typing

I'm still processing if what you told me today is real or not.

Naruk typing...

What do you want it to be?

Shekyna typing...

I want it to be real.

Naruk typing..

Why?

Shekyna typing...

Because I want you to like me. The same way I like you.

Naruk typing....

Shekyna last seen 11:38pm

A cocktail of emotions probably happening at the exact same time take turns as I look down at the text from her. She likes me too.

I hold on to the message in the textbox I am about to send her, waiting for her next appearance online. But my eyes can't keep up, they keep wondering off until its complete blackness. I fall asleep on the couch.

~~~~~~~SHEKYNA~~~~~~~

<span style="font-size:larger"><strong>M</strong></span>y eyes flip slowly in their quest to greet the rays of sun penetrating the window of my room. Groping my hand under my pillow, I search for my phone but can't find it
~~~~~~~

at the usual place. I sit up slowly, the strain on my muscles from the two hours I sat in traffic last night induces some kind of pain, I groan and stretch.

~~~~~~~~~~~~

Seventeen years ago, my father had insisted on moving his nuclear family from Nalerigu in the north to Kumasi after having landed himself a new job in the second largest city in the country. I had been excited then as I assert the city was going to be a cooler place like I hear people say. However, after having had to deal with the hectic hours in traffic, a higher cost of living and learning a completely new language from scratch, I rescinded my kind thoughts.

I do all I can to leave the hospital before 4pm to beat the long line of vehicles that tow behind each other every evening, carrying passengers in desperate need to reach their homes and set their evening agenda in motion.

Samdeen, my cousin, has been a darling in supporting us in caring for my father. Even though it was more of an extended family tradition than his sole decision, his efforts were very much appreciated. Our daily routine became popular with the nurses they begin referring to us by the shifts we run in caring for my father, he, the 'night-shift' and I, the 'day-shift'.

Unfortunately, 'night-shift' was caught up in some business yesterday while making it to the hospital. I had to stay extra five hours awaiting. My dad woke up after eight long hours worthy of a peaceful rest to a fresh pain surging from his thigh. I had to run him through the details of all that had happened, except, well, **that** part he didn't really have to hear.

My phone's battery died and I became restless at each minute that strikes on the clock. It was at eight fifteen pm that his balloon head, skin as dark as coal and extraordinarily long legs appeared behind the curtain, a smile beaming on his face, in one hand the basket of food for my father's evening meal and in the other, an
~~~~~~~~~~~~

I-phone eleven. I couldn't tell what he was smiling about after being so late, but he quickly apologized for his lateness. I didn't stand long enough to hear it. I disappeared the same minute he appeared.

The bolt ride home was exhausting. I sat on edge through it amidst impatience, restlessness and fatigue. I eventually got home. I could hear my mom on the phone with Samdeen discussing whatever the evening doctor has put him in the known about. The twins were crouched on the wine Egyptian carpet in front of the television watching a late evening show.

I shouted a 'good evening' at my mom in the room she shared with my father, I could hear her voice at an earshot from the living room, she said something in response but it didn't reach me because I was already in my room.

I pulled my phone out, thrust in the charger and took a quick shower, a shower that lasted for five minutes, seven minutes short of how long it normally took on a regular day. Today was all things but regular, had it not been the nauseating smell of the hospital my sensitive nose kept inviting long after I left there, I would not have showered at all on a day like this.

I picked up my phone which was still off, pressed hard on the power button, the uninteresting tune of Samsung galaxy S4 welcomes me to the world within my phone. I fidget with it and press 'send'. He replies were fast and spontaneous but that couldn't keep me from drifting off.

~~~~~~~~~~~~

My eyes glaze at it lying on the floor face down, I bend as I pick it up and turn it over, a smile illuminated my face at the name and texts on my screen, I bring it to my chest and hug it imaginarily.

A deafening sound robs all joy from me as my heart nearly jumps out of my chest at the reverberating sound of my alarm when it
~~~~~~~~~~~~

rings. The sudden adrenaline rush springs me. I struggle to hold my phone from falling as it bounces from finger to finger until I catch it with one hand turning the alarm off instinctively. 'Whew, What a scare!' I thought aloud. Its five am, time for the dawn prayer.

Time for dawn prayers is usually characterized by water splashing in everyone's room. I walk into my own washroom, coming out with my face, hands, arms and feet drenched.

Naza is spreading mats on a corner of the living room carved like a small mosque when I get there. The shelve carrying our holy and spiritual books sitting on the east gives the place the touch of a temple. Nagim comes in next drenched at the same parts as I am, followed by my mom. As was custom, we are all wearing veils over loose dresses completely burying our body forms, except Nagim, as we stand on the mats behind him and pray.

~~~~~~~~~

I enter the ward room, from the way I seem to be holding stares my way, I realize going an extra mile in picking out my outfit today is working. 'Are you going somewhere?' My dad asks after responding to my greeting. He is already awake at eight thirty in the morning. *Even the sick notices too.* I thought.

My cousin packs his residue and sets out as soon as I came in. My dad waves him goodbye.

'Not really.' I reply, a mild smile on my lips, while I hand him the cup of porridge I brought with me for our breakfast. He smiles and says 'thank you' while nodding in-between sips, it flatters my heart, and the feeling of being appreciated never grows old.

I'm a little shy that my father has noticed my over-board-apparel but I refuse to let it show. Rather, I drag the chair which is now used to my backside because of the countless times I've sat on it, and sit, averting my eyes from him.
~~~~~~~~~

His last seen is still 12:12 am, I can't help but wonder when his next appearance online would be. I don't want to seem desperate though there is a load sinking my heart as I delay in pressing send the 'good morning' text I have typed in the textbox. I want to ask him about so many things about himself.

The beep sound I hear anytime I receive an email chimes, I move my finger to the E-mail icon, sooner did I open the mail than I hear the familiar voice that rings almost like a melody in my ears. I leave the message, it can wait.

'Good morning, Sir. How is the pain?' The greeting is for my father but his eyes are on me. 'Good morning, doctor. I am managing. Sometimes it's more painful than other times but the medicine is helping. When I sleep, It is better.' Father emphatically responded. Naruk shifts his eyes to him and nods, 'It shall be well! We are grateful you have no underlying health conditions so your wounds are healing very fast. By early next month, you will be out of here with the way things are going.' It is my turn to smile so I do, shyly.

As he examines his wounds, his eyes whirlwind at me from time to time. I like the way he curves his lips to one side of his mouth as he smiles, it is charming. *I am charmed.*

I continue with my bizarre display of shyness until I notice him taking steps towards me, I become alert watching what he does next. He stops in front of me, gently sliding the nose-mask resting on my chin up my nasal bridge, over my mouth and nose. 'You ought to keep your mask on.' he adjusts it. 'Especially in a hospital. The virus is real and I want you safe.' I can feel the chills going down my spin, my temperature mysteriously rising.

He gives my father, who feigns oblivion to what is going on, a final nod before he starts to leave. But he stops half-way in his steps and walks back to me to whisper, 'you look stunning'. He goes. I'm hot. The air in the room is not enough for me to breath properly..

My dad is grimacing at me when I look his way, 'Do you know

him?'

I say 'Yes. He is the one who has been taking care of you.'

'I know. But he didn't see that everyone in here is not wearing their mask but you so I thought you two knew each other outside the hospital.' He says.

I reply, 'Not really. He is friendly that's why,'

'Mmm!' He skeptically moaned. 'Won't you drink your porridge? The morning is giving way to afternoon.'

Oh, yes, I haven't eaten yet. It's almost eleven thirty am.

'I will.' I say with one glance at the flasks.

'Do it now!' He commands softly.

~~~~~~~~~~~~~~~~

The porridge is hot so I leave it to cool while I go back to the message I couldn't read earlier. I'm reading it and my mouth suddenly opens to scream but it closes right back upon realizing I can't scream in the hospital. I clasp it with my hand. My chest is piling up joy. I better share the news with someone before it chokes me.

'Dad, my Visa application was approved. And the text says I should come for it in two days from now! I'm leaving for Canada for my MBA on Saturday!' I breathlessly shout the words. His reaction beats me. He laughs so loud that I am almost sure security must be on their way to us.

'Really? That scholarship you were scared to not be shortlisted for, you won and now your Visa too is ready? Grace be to the name of God!' He says this specifically to God with both hands raised and his face illuminated.

My mom appears in the moment, she heard my father, which is about all the information she needs to start jubilating.
~~~~~~~~~~~~~~~~

'Praise be to God, Praise be to God!!!!' She is more exhilarated than my dad and I combined. 'When!?' she asks in an instant.

'The Visa has been ready for days. I will travel on Saturday.' I exhalated.

'But that is too close. Today is Wednesday.' Her happiness gives way to worry.

'Then leave now and go and pack your things. You will go to your Uncle in Accra, he is going to get you prepared for your trip.' My father says pretending to not recognize the genuinty in my mother's worry.

The scholarship will last for two years, I'm going to be away for two whole years without seeing to it first that my dad is well. The hurt doubles when I remember that it will also mean going away from Naruk without a proper chance of growing our passion.

He reads my mind and says, 'Don't worry about me. We will talk everyday till the day you come back. So go now!' He's beaming in a reassuring manner. But the tears resting on my eyelids begin to fall, streaming down my face, I already miss them. *And Naruk.*

~~~~~~~~~~~

I drop by at the doctors' office on my way out, I wish I could see him, even though I don't know how to start explaining everything to him or what exactly to discuss with him. Unfortunately, 'There was an emergency surgery. This patient was badly hurt and needs thorough fixing', a nurse had told me. Such surgeries could take hours or an entire day.

As I proceed out the door, the sadness consuming me comes raining tears down my face. On-lookers shake their heads sympathetically upon seeing me. I know what they're assuming, people lose their loved ones to death every day in the hospital. They are not
~~~~~~~~~~~

entirely wrong in their thoughts, I did lose someone before he had the chance to belong to me, I lost him not to death but to fate.

~~~~~~

Saturday morning in Accra is used for practically everything else except driving to work. As early as five am, several households are up, women drying their week-long laundry behind erected walls and the streets alive with hawkers on the move to get their daily sales.

I watch from the backseat of my Uncle's car in hazy concentration on the way to the airport. Beggars come knocking on the window at the few stops we made in traffic as I look on absentmindly, hearing them without making out their words.

I had sent Naruk six long essays explaining everything to him in the bus to Accra. His video call came immediately. He was sad, I could see but also happy for me. He said two years was not going to be a big deal. He said we would keep in touch every day until I got back. 'I would wait for your return.' he had added. 'Or I might just come there if you take too long.' he even joked. It relieved me to know there still is a chance for us.

I wipe off a tear or two from my face as I watch my uncle's head dissipating out the airport entrance. We kept waving till we could see each other no more. When he is out of sight, I hold my luggage and join the queue of passengers trailing down the alley. Another tear drops.

I maneuver my way in the aisle of economy class to my seat. As I sink into it, the hollow in my chest betray any attempt to hold myself together. I put my handkerchief in my face and cry till I feel the plane taxiing on the runway. Then I raise my head and lean it on the window, looking down as the plane ascends higher and higher. 'I can't wait for the day I'll be back, until then goodbye!' I whisper to no one in particular and weep again.
~~~~~~

The End!

www.ingramcontent.com/pod-product-compliance
Lightning Source LLC
Chambersburg PA
CBHW071506150726
48000CB00006B/2724